#End
Silence

EUTON DALEY

In solidarity —
Euton Daley
Nov '23

Ending the Silence

In memory of CALVIN SIMPSON

Dedicated to
HEZEKIAH & PERNELL DALEY and KEKI SIDHWA
'immigrants' who paved the way for us and taught us
to love and believe in ourselves despite what the world
kept throwing at us. Their struggles were not in vain.

Published by Oxfordfolio
www.oxfordfolio.co.uk

© Euton Daley, 2018

Designed and typeset by Kate Kunac
Production design - Nomi Everall
Title design - Gill Jaggers
Photo credits: Book cover Jo Cox www.jocoxdesign.co.uk
all other images: David Fisher - www.fisherstudios.co.uk

ISBN 9780995679467

Printed, set and bound by Latimer Trend, Plymouth, England

AN OXFORDFOLIO PUBLICATION
www.oxfordfolio.co.uk
oxfordfolio@gmail.com

 /Oxfordfolio

 @oxfordfolio

Introduction | EUTON DALEY

Brought up by parents of the *Windrush* generation, I had a first-hand view of a race adjusting and adapting to life in a new multi-cultural Great Britain alongside inner-city race riots, communities divided by colour and limited career expectations from an inadequate school system.

This new collection, following on the heels of my new theatre production of the same title, explores an emotional and political journey of more than 200 years, spanning the parliamentary act abolishing the Transatlantic Slave Trade passed in 1807 to the establishment of the Equality and Human Rights Commission in 2007 to the present day. In all that time, how far have we come? Where are our heroes, history makers and change makers? Why are so many not recognized in the history books or halls of fame? It doesn't seek to provide answers but deals with exploring the Black diaspora experience and the struggles for justice, equality and human rights. It also tells a story of shattered dreams, resistance and aspirations, and of resilience and hope.

We become silent about things that matter
MARTIN LUTHER KING JR

Biography | EUTON DALEY

www.eutondaley.com

Euton is a theatre maker and creator, working as a producer, director, writer and performer. His practice is very much rooted in a belief in community engagement in the arts and he has passionately mentored, nurtured and supported numerous artists and young people to develop new work whilst engaging diverse audiences.

He currently develops his own work under the auspices of *Unlock the Chains Collective**. He founded the collective in 1986 to explore performance poetry as a theatrical form and to develop a dialogue with various social struggles at the time (anti-apartheid, Miners' strike, poll tax), performing at rallies, theatres and community events. The company notably had success with *Chameleon*, commissioned by Tara Arts and nominated for a London Theatre Award. Dormant for over 20 years, it reformed in 2013 when Euton left Pegasus Theatre as its Artistic Director and Chief Executive, to explore and present black experience and culture and to give Black artists a performance platform.

Euton was made an MBE in 2008 for services to the Arts and Young People. In 2013, Oxford City Council awarded him a *Certificate of Honour* for his contribution to the young people of Oxford across theatre, dance and creative learning. In 2015 he was awarded an *Honorary Fellowship* of Rose Bruford College where he studied Community Theatre Arts from 1978 to 1981.

* Original members of Unlock the Chains Collective were Yasmin Sidhwa and Calvin Simpson – both of whom I'm indebted to for the development of my take on the performance poetry genre.

4

Foreword | BEVERLEY S. HARRY

I saw it as a real coup to have a watchful eye over the stages of *#endingthesilence*, both theatrically and developmentally. Problem was however, that I then had copious amounts of material to draw from for this foreword . . . enter procrastination.

#Ending the Silence is the second of Euton's books written in a style of lyrical spoken word. It tells the story of a black man's journey growing up in England: stories of racism, discrimination, fights for equality and hope. A somewhat deeper journey from his first book, *Politics of Love*, this sophomore title exposes the familiar and unfamiliar stories of those Caribbean migrants persuaded to join Britain's post-war rebuilding programme and the experience of subsequent generations in the 'mother country'.

In the opening poem, the anthropological classification of black people 'classified at birth' is a stark reminder of why some racial groups see themselves as hierarchically superior and thus more powerful. The image of the slave boy being told to dance in one breath and then being sold in the next, reminds me of my own painful awakening having read slave journals after watching Alex Haley's *Roots*.

Similarly, on reading the complete work, it struck me that Euton's poetry is often a dismal continuum of what came before him and echoes much of what continues today . . . with a different face.

> *We wear the mask that grins and lies,*
> *It hides our cheeks and shades our eyes,—*
> *This debt we pay to human guile;*
> *With torn and bleeding hearts we smile,*
> *And mouth with myriad subtleties.*
>
> Paul Laurence Dunbar

In thinking about the direction of this foreword, I tried to circumvent listing the historical violations of civil and human rights against people of colour, however, I'm quickly reminded that people without the knowledge of their past history, origin and culture are like trees without roots. Still, Marcus Garvey's words may not give me carte blanche to do so but, it hopefully sets a curiosity in the reader.

#endingthesilence also addresses the egregious acts of gun violence and personalizes the debate, "here I stand with a gun in my hand and I don't know what to do . . .". The poetic license Euton takes here transports the reader into the evolving quagmire in which young black men often find themselves today. Can I say government sanctioned cultural genocide? Whilst unfixing the ideas and imagery in my head to parchment, events surrounding the subjugation of black people was again in the news. Protestations of #blacklivesmatter were again leading black people to the question-would the white policemen have shot and killed an unarmed white man, this time in his own backyard reaching for his iPhone?

But this book is not solely about the experience of the Melanin rich, and the theatrical performances didn't answer the many questions posted about their experiences of social and civil injustices. It's a poetic journey. What makes this book a worthy read is the sad reality that, as the world commemorates the 50th anniversary of the Reverend Dr Martin Luther King's "I have a dream" speech, people continue to be judged by the colour of their skin rather than the content of their character.

Like many revolutionary poets, Euton's work is inspirational, frustrating, powerful and engaging. Often you begin to chant the rhythms of justice, freedom, equality and at other times you are silently reading waves of impassioned poetry setting a multiplicity of scenarios. I know this much is true, you will be moved one way or another by reading #endingthesilence

I have been locked by the lawless.
Handcuffed by the haters.
Gagged by the greedy.
And, if I know anything at all,
It's that a wall is just a wall
and nothing more at all.
It can be broken down.
Assata Shakur

Beverley Harry is a college lecturer specializing in US/UK Politics and Sociology. She is also the founder and director of the Miss P Foundation, a local fundraising charity offering financial support to young people in the Arts.

The Poems

PART 3 | #HOPE

Prologue

KNOWLEDGE

I know what I know at this present time
In a few moments it could be less than what I previously knew
Which could be more
For this little knowledge
May be of greater use to me
Than the vast knowledge that I used to know.

Hold fast to dreams
for if dreams die, life is a broken
winged bird that cannot fly
LANGSTON HUGHES

PART 1:
#BLACKLIVESMATTER

An historical reflection juxtaposed with
modern day resistance, protest and struggle

Until the lion tells his side of the story
Tales of the hunt will always glorify the hunter
AFRICAN PROVERB

Classified

Classified / Classified
Classified at birth / Black
Classified at birth / Coloured
Classified at birth / Heathens
Classified / Classified
Kaffir! Coolie! Nigger! Boy!
Yes, Sir! No, Sir!
Classified / Going! Going! Gone!
Classified / SOLD
Classified / Classified
Classified at birth
The Limbo dancer
Always going under
Always / Going under

Classified at work / In schools
Classified on the streets / Where we live
Where's your passbook, Boy?
Passbook, Boy!
Classified NOT White

Classified / Classified
Classified
The ape / the baboon / the monkey up the tree
Play the fiddle / IT WILL dance the tune
Let's see you dance, Boy!
Dance Boy!

Classified BEFORE birth

England

Slowly
Oh too slowly
Beginning
Beginning
We're beginning to understand
The rules of this ya place
England
All the lies them a feed
Till we starve ourselves
The hate them a feel
Notions of superiority
What's mine is yours
Is the doctrine that you teach
But what's yours is yours
Is the practice that you preach
Mash it up!
You hear me
Tek not talk!

Justice! Freedom! Equality!
Justice! Freedom! Equality! (I like the sound a dat!)
Justice! Freedom! Equality!
Justice! Freedom! Equality! (I'll have some a dat!)

Justice? Freedom? Equality?
Justice? Freedom? Equality?
Words them a use
To keep I down
Words!

We need words to educate
Words to liberate
Not words to enslave
Nor words that proclaim blame
Angry words
Resentful words

Words
You chew them up
Spit them out
As gospel
Tablets of stone
Declaration
Demarcation
Of our race
In this ya place
England
Words them a use
To keep I down
Mash it up!
Educate them
And not just with words!

200 Years

Repatriation/No closure
Reparation/No closure
Colonization/No closure
Enslavement/No closure
40 acres and a mule/No closure
Over 200 years/And still No closure
No closure
200 years of hurt/No apologies
200 years of memories/No acknowledgement

Stolen lands of Africa/No closure
Killing fields in the Caribbean/No closure
Blood spilt on the streets/No closure
Death in police custody/No closure
Tazered/No closure
Over 200 years/And still No closure
No closure
200 years of hurt/No apologies
200 years of memories/No acknowledgement
No closure/over 200 years
And still no closure
200 Years
No Closure.

Too Long

Oh Brother, Oh Sister
What's/wrong with us
Sitting at the back a
Sitting at the back a
Oh Brother, Oh Sista
What's/wrong with us
Sitting at the back a de bus

Stop/sitting at the back a
Stop/sitting at the back a
Oh Brother, Oh Sista
What's/wrong with us
Stop/sitting at the back a de bus

Too long/too long
For far too long
A weeping and a wailing
A longing and a wanting
Too long/too long
For far too long

Too long/too long
Too long/for far too long
The dangling of the noose
The crack of the whip
The butt of the gun
For far too long/too long
Yes sir/no sir/thank you sir
Docile/For far too long

Too long/too long
Too long! Too long!
For far too long
Rise up/Wise up
Rise up/Wise up
Rise up!

The System

The rich gets richer
And the poor poorer
This injustice won't ever cease
It's the heart of this wretched system
In which the poor
Fight and die

But don't shed no tears
Don't shed no tear
It shall cease
It
Shall cease!

No Blacks, No Irish, No Dogs

Doors / Open
Doors / Close
Doors / Open
Doors / Close
Doors / Closing
Doors / Closing
Doors / Closing

Breathe / 2,3,4
Breathe / 2,3,4
Doors / Closing
Doors / Closing
Doors / Closing
Doors / Close

(Sighs)

Keep knocking
Knocking
Knocking
Breathing
Sighing
Breathing
Knocking
Keep knocking

Doors / Keep closing
(sighs)
We know you can hear
We know you're there
Doors / Closing
Doors / SLAMMED!

Do we keep knocking?
Make a fuss?
Leave?
Ram it down?
Breathe /
Breathe /
Doors / Closing
Doors / Closing
Doors / Closing
Doors /
CLOSED!

"It's nothing to do with me!"

We a take the pressure
In this snake ridden pit
And you just sit
And say
"It's nothing to do with me!"
"It's nothing to do with me!"

While they beat us
And kill us
Ban us and exploit us
You just . . .
"It's nothing to do with me!"
"It's nothing to do with me!"

"It's nothing to do with me!"
If only I had that luxury to say
"It's nothing to do with me!"
"It's nothing to do with me!"

We a hold out our hands
We a plea for help/Petitions/Debates
We a hold out our hand
We a plea for help/Sanctions/Boycotts
Where do we go from here?
Petitions, Debates/Sanctions, Boycotts
Petitions, Debates/Sanctions, Boycotts
Petitions, Debates/Sanctions, Boycotts
Petitions, Debates/Sanctions, Boycotts

Some say / Guns!

"It's/Nothing to do with me!"
"It's nothing to do with me!"

But where do we go from here
"It's nothing to do with me!"
Where do we go from here?
"It's nothing to do with me!"
Surely, we must resist
Defend ourselves?
We lobby / We march
We march / We chant
We pray / We advocate for change
The ballot box making no difference.
We scrabble and fight amongst ourselves
We fight for survival
We fight for existence
Continually counting the loss of lives
So yes / Guns!
"That's/Definitely nothing to do with me!"
"Absolutely/Nothing to do with me!"

We a take the pressure
In this snake ridden pit
And you just sit
And say
It's nothing to do with me
It's nothing to do with me!

State of Emergency: Riot Act – Part 1

Here me a stand
With a gun in me hand
And I don't know
I don't know
And I don't know what to do

Got caught up in the commotion
And I don't know what to do
You see
Dem charge from the front
Dem charge from the back
Cylinders on full throttle
Dem launch them attack
And what a commotion!
And I don't know
I don't know
And I don't know what to do

A peaceful protest
Please don't shoot
I'm law abiding
Please don't shoot
Just want human rights and justice
So please
Don't shoot!

PLEEASSEEE
DON'T SHOOT!

Such a waste of human life
Mutilation of body and mind
The prey
The victims
The old cliché
This world is so unkind

Another shot
A piercing cry
Another dies
And I don't know
I don't know
And I don't know what to do

And the joy on their faces
As the kick and the fist
And the baton and the gun
Rage in

And I don't know
And I don't know
And I don't know what to do

What good are bricks and stones
Sticks and bottles
What good are
Words and pleas for mercy
How did it begin
When will it end?

And I don't know
And I don't know
And I don't know what to do

NOOOOO
DON'T SHOOT

You stupid fool
You've killed him
G'me the blasted gun
You've played right into their hands
More shootings
More deaths
Can't you understand?

And for each tear
They abandoned the law
For each drop of blood
All sanity is lost

And I don't know
And I don't know
And I don't know what to do

Then
Dem regroup from the front
Dem regroup from the back
Cylinders on full throttle
Dem relaunch dem attack
A brand new commotion!
And here I stand
With this gun in me hand
And I don't know
And I don't know
And I don't know
What to do

Welcome to South Africa

Welcome!
Welcome!
Welcome to South Africa
Welcome to South Africa
Welcome to South Africa
You're all welcome to South Africa!
There's no Apartheid
That's in the past
You're ALL/ Welcome to South Africa

Welcome to the land/of Milk and Honey
Welcome to the land/where it's always sunny!
Diamonds and gold/ Riches untold
Nuclear capability/IF necessary
The Man from Delmonte says/Yes!
Welcome to South Africa
Welcome to South Africa
Welcome!

Welcome
Welcome to a state of emergency
Distortion of facts and statistics/Of reality

Welcome to routine investigations
Corruption and conspiracy
Widespread torture
Detention of the innocent

Welcome to malnutrition and poverty
Forced removals

Injustices
Inadequate education
Enshrined in laws and regulations

Welcome to confrontation
Destruction of life
Militarization, a battlefield
In this land of milk and honey
Where we never see the god-damn money
Except when it's used
In the form of
Oppression
Repression
And suppression
Against us

We're doing our best
I've given my word
Changes take time
Haven't you heard?

We've heard
We've heard

We've heard/Bullets and tanks
Teargas and batons
We've heard/Barking dogs
Loudspeakers and warnings
We've heard/Screams
Of children crying
People dying/In the townships
The gold mines
We've heard

We've heard
Propaganda / Slogans and lies
And pontification

We've heard
Yes, we've heard
In the hotels / The restaurants
We've heard
We've heard
The respectability of apartheid
We've heard

Well, there's no point talking to this one
Educate them and look what happens!
And to think we could have made him an honorary white!
Doesn't matter what he says, he's still a Kaffir
Give them a microphone
A platform
And they don't half go on!

Well my son
The argument is not who was here first
It's a question of advancing civilization

Welcome / To South Africa!

State of Emergency: Riot Act – Part 2

If I was to bleed
As I often do
And you my Bassie/Mr Boss Man
Was to bleed
As one day you're going to!
What will I find?
White blood
Or will it be black?
Neither, but the same I think
So tell me
How will you begin
To classify that?

My thesis could be wrong
Let me see
Let's clear up this
Little mystery

(reader aims a gun/weapon)

So, what will I find
In this superior blood of yours?
Red/red, red blood!
Same as mine
Same as the sea of red
The lives of countless
Brothers and Sisters
Spilled
Simple because of the colour of their skin

Because of your notion of Black = inferior
That our lives do not matter.
Your life in remembrance
Of those long gone?
The thought keeps crossing my mind
Fortunately for you
It would not begin
To atone for the atrocities
The genocide
So, before my blood boils
RED
Get out of my sight

Shoo!
SHOO!

R.I.P

Why / Why are our parents buying their children
Why / Why
Why

I know / I know
We know
There must be a better way
To live
To value life
To love
And be loved
A better quality of life
So why / Why
Why

Why / Why do all our heroes die

Why
Why / Why do all our heroes die
Imprisoned
Impoverished
Why
Why / Why do all our heroes die
Young
Why
Why / Why do all our heroes die
In vain?

21st Century Tomfoolery

Tomorrow will be a day/a day like any other day
Today somebody else's child/tomorrow it could be mine
Today we'll talk and make demands
Tomorrow we'll bury our dead
For tomorrow will be a day/a day like any other day
Bullets echoing death/victims fall in pools of blood
Today somebody else's child/tomorrow it could be mine
Tomorrow will be a day/a day like any other day
We'll send men to the moon/and back again
Whilst queues at food banks continue to grow
With technology pin-pointing
Destroying targets thousands of miles away
But we're still without the basic need for clean water for everyone
Tomorrow will be a day/a day like any other day
Spending billions on trident and nuclear weapons
Yet where are the shelters for the homeless
The living wage for all
Why do so few have so many/Whilst so many have so few
Tomorrow you'll launch another judicial enquiry
Today you'll pass another bill of law
Whitewashing over the cracks
Today we're clearly not your priority
Tomorrow we'll expect more of the same
Pieces of a dream/it all seems real
These pieces of a dream/this nightmare
Our eyes have been tinted
We're beginning to live the lie
That only God knows the reason

Why we live or die

We won't cover up the scars/let the whole world see

The deeds of civilized men

Don't cover up the scars/let the whole world know

The deeds of civilized men

Pieces of a dream/it all seems real

These pieces of a dream/this nightmare

Tomorrow will be a day/a day like any other day

Today somebody else's child/tomorrow it could be mine

Tomorrow will be a day

A day

Like any other day

Journey Home

Our dream is to fly
Over the rainbow
Rise up! Rise up! Rise up!
Spread your broken wings
And fly to the Heavens
Rise up! Rise up! Rise up!
Soar amongst the Gods
Taste the sweet smell of victory

Rise up! Rise up! Rise up
Rise up! Rise up! Rise up

Bathe in the waters of Freedom
Cleanse from this life
Bathe in the waters of Freedom
Cleanse / From this life
Bathe in the waters of Freedom
Cleanse from this life
Cleanse / Waters of Freedom
Cleanse / Waters of Freedom
Cleanse / Waters of Freedom
Freedom
Freedom

PART 2:
#WALKINGONEGGSHELLS

Personal struggles, stories and
perspectives on surviving

*We can let our experiences define us
or choose to define our experiences*

Awakening

Breathe
Got to / Got to
Got to
Breathe
Break through the barriers
Come up for air
Breathe
Got to
Got to
Got to /
Breathe

Childhood

I cry me to sleep
Sleep
Never to wake
To wake
Never to wake
To hear birds sing
Nor see the sun rise
Or set

Never to wake
To look at Mama
Struggling with seven children
In her arms
On her lap
At her feet

Never to wake
To watch Pa
With his pipe mopin' round the house
Drunk
When he was there
Drunk
When he wasn't there

Never to wake
To watch
Sister setting off each morning
No words were spoken

But we all knew
And the younger ones
And I
Watched and envied

Never to wake
To wake
To watch
Children on the streets
Kicking stones
The sound of their laughter
Barking dogs at their heels
The empty contented
Smiles on their faces

Never to wake
To wake
To cry for my brothers and sisters
My mothers and my fathers
Nor to hear
The sound or see the drops
Of their tears
Crying for me

I cry me to sleep
Never to wake
Never
Never to wake.

Lament

Feeling restless
Never succeeding
Needing aspiration
Itching to get out
Confinement. Black.
Hungry for acceptance
Longing for dignity
Peace of mind
Praying. Freedom
Wanting protection
Longing
For dignity
Wishing love
But feeling resentment
Seeing hate
Always restless
Wanting assurance
An easier life

We a hungry
We a thirsty
For acceptance
Confinement. Confirmed.

Rivers of Babylon

By the Rivers of
By the Rivers of
By the Rivers of Babylon
I found a little time to contemplate
I found a little time to shed a tear
By the Rivers of
By the Rivers of
By the Rivers of Babylon
I found a little time to pray

By the Rivers of
By the Rivers of
By the Rivers of Babylon
I found a little time to grieve
I found a little time to hear
I found a little time
I found a little time for me
By the Rivers of
By the Rivers of
By the Rivers of Babylon
I found a little strength to carry on
By the Rivers of
By the Rivers of
By the Rivers of Babylon
I found a little time/to dance

Letter from the Edge

Mama
Dear Mama
You've inspired me
To dream
To think
You've always said
When you feel it / speak it
For all to hear
Loud and clear

Well, Mama
Dear Mama
I spoke it and felt it
The silence
That amplified sound
The heart beating
Pounding
Thoughts
Racing
Chasing
Each other round the brain
The tension
The pain
No rest

No rest
But I'm not wicked!
I've thought good thoughts

Done good deeds
Sleepless nights
Tired days
Tired
Always tired
Tired of being tired
Weary
Restless dreams
Ageing before my time

Mama
Dear Mama
We're struggling
I'm struggling
Still stumbling through
Fighting
Always fighting
Mama
Dear Mama
It won't be long now
I feel it
See you soon

Drifting

Drifting
Drifting

Drifting
On a timeless raging ocean
Looking for calm
Looking for solace

Drifting
Like a spec in a vast void
Strangers in our own lands
Drifting
Dreaming of hope
Dreaming of tomorrow

Dreaming of hope
Dreaming of tomorrow

Drifting
On ever shifting sand
Of politician speeches
Never settled
Never sure
Diseased
Homeless
Stateless
The only certainty?
Many more of us will die

Drifting
Once there was hope
Now only doubt
Drifting
Fragile existence
Fragile state of mind

Drifting
Off course
Drifting
Off the off course
Drifting
And dying in the ghettoes
The townships
The favelas
Reservations
The inner cities

Drifting
Dreaming of hope
Dreaming of tomorrow

Dreaming of hope
Dreaming of tomorrow

Drifting
On the edge
And living on borrowed time

Drifting
Hoping
Praying
"Our Father which art in Heaven"

Drifting
Dreaming of hope
Dreaming of tomorrow
Dreaming of hope
Dreaming of tomorrow
Dreaming of hope
Dreaming of tomorrow
Dreaming
Dreaming
Dreaming
Drifting
On empty dreams
Empty
Dreams

Cleansing

Run.
Run, Run, Run, Run
Run child
Run

Run
With the wind
To your back
Run.
Run, Run, Run, Run
Run
As fast
As hard as you can
Run
Towards the sun
Rays welcoming
Run.

Run
Leap barbed wire fences
Enemies entrenched
Like your fore-fathers and mothers
Before you
Run.
When the shots ricocheted
From steel barrels
When the whips cracked
We ran. We ran

On seeing the signs
No Niggers
No Blacks
Whites Only
We've been running ever since

Run
Run child
Run
No need to look
To see
You know
The icy cold stares of injustice

Run.
Run, Run, Run, Run
Run child
Run
Fire burns
The rage of hate
Run
Leave the past behind you
Run.
Chaos and destruction
Remains
Crows hovering
Devouring
A society
Decaying
A graveyard
Run.

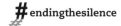

Run child
Run
Run with all your might
Run
The martyrs
Whose foundation is now your guiding path
The future beckons
Run
On the wind of change
Run.
Run.
You're falling
Falling
No! No!
Run.
Run
Run.
Run, Run, Run, Run
Run child
Run.

Run.
Survive
Survive
Run
You have to
We have to
Run
Run
And when you can't run
Anymore

Crawl

Crawl

Crawl

From childhood to adulthood

I've been naked

And couldn't protect myself

Run

From childhood

I've been running

To adulthood

Run

To survive

To live another day

To rise

One by one

Run

Run.

Run, Run, Run, Run

Run child

RUN

Pretence *

The P
The P
The Pre
The Pre
The Pretence
The Pretence is
The Pretence is wearing
The Pretence is wearing thin

The Pretence is wearing thin
In this green and pleasant land
No room to move
No room to breathe
In this green and
In this green and
In this green and pleasant land
Can't play the game
Won't achieve the fame
In this green and
In this green and
In this green and pleasant land

The Pretence is wearing thin
The Pretence is wearing thin

I want to push
To scream and shout
Let it all out

In this green and
In this green and
In this green and pleasant land
In this green
And pleasant land

Suffocating
Dying
Before my time
In this green and pleasant land

Eyes
Constantly watching
In this green and pleasant land
Alone
Basking
In the heat of their stares
Piercing
Burning
In this green and pleasant land
On trial
In this green and
In this green and
No room to move
No room to breathe
And I can't keep it up
I can't keep it up
I can't
In this green and
In this green and
In this green and pleasant land

The Pretence is wearing thin
The Pretence is wearing thin
The Pretence is wearing
The Pretence is
The Pretence is
The Pretence
The Pretence
The Pre
The Pre
The P
The P
P
P
P
P

* Written in collaboration with Yasmin Sidhwa
for her one woman play *Chameleon*

Preacher Man —
These are the Days

Another day another dollar
But the dollar
Won't keep the family
Outta the squalor
So every day you hear
The holler, holler
Hollering
Screams
Of children
Crying
Dying
Dying
Crying

These are the days
These are the days

Dem smash down you door and shoot you up
Lock you in a cell and beat you up
You a walk down the road
And dem pick you up for SUS
Doesn't justice stand for all?
These are the days of who can you trust

These are the days
Of third world politics
These are the days

When dem think dem have all the tricks

These are the days
These are the days

These are the days
Of conformity and collusion
These are the days
Of living in a meagre existence

These are the days
Yes, these are the days

These are the days
When money talks
And with the gun, rules
These are the days

These are the days
When the haves and the have nots
Converse no more
'Cause one got too much
The other not enough
And each holding on to what dem have

These are the days of a credit society
Living in a plastic economy
Borrowing to repay
What was borrowed
To repay what was borrowed
To repay what was borrowed

To repay. . . chu!

These are the days
Yes, these are the days
Nations, having many possessions
But owning very little
Poisoned by self-preservation
Seeing only what dem want to see
Short-sightedness

These are the days
Yes, these are the days

And when dem decide to press the button
Dem will be safe, the rest of us forgotten
Dem will be safe, the rest of us forgotten

So where are the voices of liberation
'Cause no one's safe
Freeee
So we better ALL be aware
Of what's going on

These are the days
Yes, these are the days
Fight back
Fight back
Fight back

In Emergency: Break Glass

Close your eyes

Close your eyes

Close your eyes
Close your eyes
Take a deep breath
Think
Make yourself invisible
Think!
Ho-ho hold
Hold the anger back.

Hold the anger back
Not in shame
I have nothing to hide
But out of fear
You hold the anger back
Just, just
Hold the anger back
Ho-ho hold
Hold the anger back

Hold the anger back
A say, hold the anger back
It's not a question of right or wrong
You just

Hold the anger back
Stop. Think
Take a deep breath
No more tears to be shed
No more blood flow from these vein
Ho-ho hold
Hold the anger back
Hold the anger back

When the rude boys attack
For the umpteenth time
And you scream for the umpteenth time
And the neighbours
Behind their net curtain barricades
Choose not to hear
Won't hear
Don't hear
Or just don't care
And the passers-by
Don't stop
Call for help
Nor mutter placating words
You just
Hold the anger back
Hold the anger back
When the institutions
Conceive to block each and every avenue
And everyone accepts
That's the way of the world
And when you cry to your friends
And their only sympathy

Is to let out a sigh
You just
Hold the anger back
Yes, hold the anger back

When the colour of one's skin
Is your identity badge
You want to shout
I'm not just a colour
A statistic
I have a name
And my name is
My name is
My name is
Hold the anger back
Hold the anger back

Ho-ho hold
Hold the anger back
Don't be intimidated
They mustn't have the privilege
Don't show the hurt
Or the hatred
That you feel inside
Hold the anger back
With dignity
Hold the anger back
It mustn't be allowed to eat you up
Let it give you new strength
With each and every blow
Take a deep breath

Bide your time
Hold the anger back
Just, just hold the anger back
Hold the anger back
Yes, yes, Ho-ho-hold
Ho-ho-hold
Hold the anger back
Hold the anger back

IN EMERGENCY: BREAK GLASS

Screams – long and piercing

Hungry Heart

A hungry heart
Is a painful heart
Is a troublesome heart
Is a powerful heart
A powerful heart
A powerful heart

Without food in them belly
       How can they fight
Without food in them belly
       How can they think
Without food in them belly
       How can they live
Without food in them belly
       Another nation in debt
To the West
To the West
To the West
To the West

When we gonna get
       Some food inna belly
When we gonna get
       Some peace of mind
When we get that
       Peace in our belly
Then we gwan get
       Some thoughts in our mind

A hungry heart
Is a painful heart
Is a troublesome heart
Is a powerful heart
A powerful heart
A powerful heart

The heart will remember
          The toiling and sorrow
The heart will remember
          The suffering and strain
The heart will remember
          Been used and abused
The heart will remember
          Degradation and pain

When we gonna get
          Some release from these sorrows
When we gonna get
          Some rest along the way
When we gonna stop
          This toiling and struggle
When we gwan see
          Our people gain

When we gonna
When we gonna
When we gonna see our people gain

When we gonna
When we gonna

When we gonna see our people gain
When we gonna see
When we gonna see
When we gonna see our people gain

When we gonna see our people gain

A hungry heart
Is a painful heart
Is a troublesome heart
Is a powerful heart
A powerful heart
A powerful heart

Repercussions

When WORDS / mask the answers
And don't make a difference
Regardless of their legal binding status
When TEARS / are not enough
Even though they keep flowing, raining
Gushing – can't stem the tide

When HATRED / has taken root
Buried deep, cancerous, maligned
Indeed, critically dangerous
When GRIEF / rips another family apart
Its frequency numbs and divides a community
Into self-preservation
Into – non-action
Into – acceptance

When JUSTICE / doesn't prevail
And we're no longer the media headlines
The politicians' election card
When FREEDOM / such a distant memory
Yet somehow etched in the memory DNA
Of something that was important
But has long since been forgotten

When PRAYERS / receive no answers
Even for the staunch believer
The hardened follower
When all HOPE / is gone

All strength to fight / drained
Like water sucked from the seas
Clouds pulled from the skies

When all that is left are / UNRECORDED HISTORIES
Dying with the passing of each Elders
When the next generation / BURDENED
WITH EXPECTATIONS
Realizing they / YOU,
Like our parents before us
Can't fulfill the dream
Indeed, when all HOPE / is gone
What is left / but EXTINCTION
The DEATH / of a race

When all HOPE / WHEN ALL HOPE IS GONE

Sign of the Times

You say / You say / You say
You say I'm opinionated
Demanding
Always seem to have a chip on my shoulder
Walking around as if the world owes me big time
Attitudinally / Angry
Argumentatively / Aggressive

Well / I'm not going to tell you otherwise
But hope my words enlighten
Inform.
Don't know where / Don't know how
How to even begin.
Let's start at the end
To somehow get to the beginning.

It's like / It's like / It's like
It's like / If I were you
I might be able to say
Never ever have I / Never ever have I
Had children pointing and laughing at me
Or crying and running to hide due to the colour of my skin
Never ever have I / Never ever have I
Been told *we don't want your sort round here*
Never ever have I / Never ever have I
Been called names
Often prefaced by the word *black*
Or ending with *Nigger*

Never ever have I / Never ever have I
Been followed / pursued as soon as I walk into a shop
And when next! somehow doesn't mean you
Waiting patiently next in line
And never ever have I / Never ever have I
Had to make sure I have kept the receipt
However small the purchase
Even for 20p.
Too many CCTV / conveniently /
Don't work when you need them!

Never ever?
Never ever! Never ever!
Never ever?
Never ever!

Never ever have I / Never ever have I
In applications lied about who I am / And where I'm from
Perfecting a voice
That hides any traces that would hinder
A pathway to the next stage
Never ever have I / Never ever have I
Been greeted / Betrayed / with *Oh, I wasn't expecting you!*
When eventually we meet
Never ever have I / Never ever have I
Been cruised by a squad car, stopped / Searched / Detained
Imprisoned / Consistently
Racially profiled / Falsely / Wrongly / Allegedly
Never ever have I / Never ever have I
Been wrestled to the ground / Unnecessarily
And end up unconscious / Dead

There and them / Or later in police custody
Never ever have I / Never ever have I
Lived in fear of that knock on the door
Or having doors slammed in your face

Never ever?
Never ever! Never ever!
Never ever?
Never ever!

Never ever have I / Never ever have I
Been shackled and bound
Whipped and beaten like an animal
Never ever have I / Never ever have I
Been spoken to or treated as a child
Referred to as *boy*
When I have grown-up children of my own
Never ever have I / Never ever have I
Been spat at / Shot at / For a laugh / For sport

Never ever?
Never ever! Never ever!
Never ever?
Never ever!

Never ever have I / Never ever have I
Had to sit at the back of the bus
Or by toilets in restaurants
And never ever have I / Never ever have I
Thank God / had to stand in *Blacks Only* queues
Never ever have I / Never ever have I

Been bartered/Traded/Sold
Goods to the highest bidder
Remaining unsalaried, low paid
Working non-stop to make a living
Never ever have I/Never ever have I
Been intimidated by the cracking of a whip
Burning effigies
The butt of a gun
Tortured/Maimed/Beaten/Shot at, again/Burnt alive
Never ever have I/Never ever have I
Had my people swung from a noose
Ropes dangling from trees
Or dragged along dirt roads tied to the back of pick-up trucks

Never ever?
Never ever! Never ever!
Never ever?
Never ever!

Never ever?
Never ever! Never ever!
Never ever?
Never ever!

You see/You see/You see
You see/I have forever had
To worry about daily survival
Body /Soul/Mind
Forever needing to/Belong
To belong/to belong/to belong
To not be invisible

From generation to generation
Who's to say what post-traumatic *slave-disorders*
Hasn't been passed through these genes
Resulting in my attitudinally angry posture
Who's to say!
You see / You see / You see
Living in the present
Is forever living with the past
Forever ever?
Hope not!
Or YOU may never stop saying
We're opinionated / Argumentative / Aggressive . . .
Do we need to continue . . . ?
Do we need to!

Knowing your Enemies

God!
You are my witness
I can't run anymore
And God!
Be my witness
There's nowhere else to hide

In desperation
I plea to thee
Help us
Deliverance
Is all we ask

And God!
The hundreds of years
Have proved our existence
So don't ask me to beg

Is there no place in Heaven for us?
Are you too part of the conspiracy
Building the walls
Brick by brick
Erecting the fence
Strand by strand?

Answer me!

God!
You too have witnessed
And God!
You too have remained
Silent
Silent
Silent

PART 3:
#HOPE

Dreams, aspirations and looking forward

If you want to go quickly, go alone
If you want to go far, go together
AFRICAN PROVERB

Ending the Silence

The wind blows
The barren soil
Across the barren landscape
Winter came early
As usual
Summer
Hardly at all
No one smiled
No laughter
No one groaned
Nor moaned
The faint
Muffled sound of children
Crying of hunger
Dying of hunger
Of thirst
Is lost
In the wind
In the cold
Who would care anyway
If the muffled could be heard
If the gag was removed
We are suffering
In silence
Living on the edge
And wasting away
Another generation
Left
To rot
In this conspiracy
Of silence
Silence
Silence
Silence
Silence

Voices

Voices
I hear
Voices
In my head

I hear voices in my head
I hear voices
      Remember
In my head
      Remember

Voices
I hear
Voices
In my head

      Remember your history
      Don't let it
      Don't let it
      Repeat itself

      Remember the history
      Of past and present
      Remember the history
      Not told in books
      Remember the history
      Of broken promises
      The rape of our bodies

Our lands

Remember
Generations
Living empty lives
Remember
Don't let it repeat itself
Remember
Don't let it repeat itself
Don't let it /
Repeat itself
Remember

I hear voices in my head
I hear voices in my head

Have you come to help me?
Have you come to deliver me free?
Come on, take these chains
Release me
Release me
From captivity

When will we learn
The bond that holds you is yourself
Cannot unlock chains that are not there
Unlock the thoughts that are in your mind
Don't live in ignorance and fear

I hear voices in my head
I hear voices in my head
I hear
Voices

In my head

Release me
Release me

      Unlock the chains
      Unlock the chains
      Unlock
      Unlock
      Unlock the chains

      Unlock the chains
      The chains
      Chains of captivity

      Unlock the chains
      The chains
      Chains of mental torture

      Unlock the chains
      And learn
      Unlock the chains
      And live
      Unlock the chains
      And be free

I hear voices in my head
I hear voices in my head
I hear
Voices
      Break the chains!

Strength of a Nation

All alone was I
Living in vain / From day to day
Confused / Frustrated
No hope / No future
No future / No world

No hope / No future
No future / No world
No hope

(Drums)

Then the inspiration came
Like a crystal light to guide
Penetrating / Through my soul
I felt that beat / That pulse
That heartbeat

We struggle / In hope
We die / For a cause
We struggle / In hope
To survive / For a future

For no matter what them take
Them can't take away
That beat / That pulse
That dread dread beating
Of the drums

All alone was I

No more
No more
I felt that beat
That pulse
That heartbeat
Of a nation

To the beat / To the beat
To the beat / To the beat
To the dread dread beating
Of the drums

To the beat / To the beat
To the beat / To the beat
To the dread dread beating
Of the drums

Children of a Lesser God

Don't wanna be
Don't wanna be
Don't wanna be no

    Train or bus driver
    Dub poet, hip hop rapper, grime or
    Lyrical gangster

Don't wanna be no

    Sprinter, long distance runner
    Boxer, basketball, fleet of foot shuffler

Don't wanna be no

    Hospital janitor, porter, nurse
    Office cleaner, factory worker

Don't wanna be no

    Drug dealer, ganja smoking dude
    Reggae, sound system, DJ, Beats man

Don't wanna be no

    High five, hand slapping
    Lips cussing, teeth hissing
    Ignorant immigrant

Wake up everybody
Time to rise and shine
Open your eyes
To the possibilities

    You see
    Your expectation of me is limited
    And limiting
    Highly educated, articulate and intelligent
    Yet street-wise enough
    To not let YOUR Education
    Turn me into no damn fool!

Don't believe
Don't believe
Don't believe the hype
Too many of us can testify
That THAT certificate, however high the grade,
Will do little to how they see or treat you
Still a commodity
Having relatively no value or life
Beyond being bought and sold
And whilst I may not be
The next Prime Minister
Manager of England cricket or football teams
No high court judge,
Oscar winning stage or movie star
Your expectation lacks ambition
And is devoid of imagination

Fulfill your potential
Don't let others define you
Have ambition
Be who you wanna be

Who you wanna be
But you're good at sport, fond of music,
are a great dancer!
Why don't you choose from those skills set!?
I don't know what I wanna be
But I do know that I don't wanna be

Don't wanna be no

No long distant runner, sprinter, limbo dancer
So I blank you
Shut you, and your well-intentioned
Career advice, DOWN
My expectations are greater than yours

This essay, for example, comes
With distinction! A-star-plus!
I'm looking up whilst you're looking down
On an uppity-little-Black-16-year-old boy
From the wrong side of town
Another angry black man
A problem that needs to be dealt with
For I'm refusing to conform
To an education system
That educates me to know my place

Wake up everybody
Time to rise and shine
Open your eyes
To the possibilities

You see
The images that we see affect
Who we become
The words we use can aspire and inspire
I'm changing the default from white
No longer subscribing to the notion
That we're Children of a Lesser God
A minority
Knowledge is power
And until real change has taken place
I'm gonna be rebellious
Forever angry
A rule breaker
Game changer
New world maker
Create the world YOU want to live in

Fulfill your potential
Don't let others define you
Have ambition

Be who you wanna be

Strive to be the best at whatever you do

If I wanna be
If I wanna be
If I wanna be a

Train or bus driver
Dub poet, hip hop rapper, grime or
Lyrical gangster

If I wanna be a

Sprinter, long distance runner
Boxer, basketball, fleet of foot shuffler

If I wanna be a

Hospital janitor, porter, nurse
Office cleaner, factory worker

If I wanna be a

Drug dealer, ganja smoking dude
Reggae, sound system, DJ, Beats man

If I wanna be a

Some high five, hand slapping
Lips cussing, teeth hissing
Ignorant immigrant

If I wanna be

It will be from choice
MY choice
Not from your narrow definition of me

Wake up everybody
Time to rise and shine
Wake up everybody
Time to shine, shine, shine

Time to SHINE

Hope

Hope

Hope

Hope

So much hangs/On such a small word
Such a small word/Yet filled
With so much/Promise
So Much/Hope!

Hope
　　　　Hope gives rise to possibilities
Hope
　　　　Hope provides a sense of purpose
Hope
　　　　Is that thing which makes you face each and every day

To Hope/Is to dream
To Hope/Is to have faith
That NOT everything in life is Black & White/white or wrong
That the grass is NOT greener on the other side
That politicians CAN be truthful
To hope is to SEE the bombs
Behind the platitudes and rhetoric
To hope/is to believe
That others WILL believe/WILL follow
And that WE/The People
CAN/we the People WILL make a difference.

But/Beware!
To Hope implies to take action
To do something
It relies on a different mindset
Therefore, it takes effort
To Hope is hard work
It requires a *Can Do/Will Do* attitude
It requires patience and impatience
Tact and diplomacy
That we see the glass as half full not half empty
And that we give selflessly to others without thoughts of personal gain

So be prepared to graft
For such a small word
It is often hard to achieve
BUT to NOT try is not worth contemplating

To Hope/is to be optimistic
To Hope/is to look to the future
To Hope/is to dream
To Hope/is to believe

I NEED YOU to Hope
Hope prepares you for battles with the enemy
Hope allows you to fight back even against gigantic odds
Hope enables you to strive and to thrive

Hope is enlightenment
So breathe!
Fill your thoughts with a thousand hopes
For hope induces self-respect
Dignity

Pride

When a nation lives in Hope
Hope echoes across the land
And a great rejoicing is felt
For then we truly believe

To Hope/is to dream
To believe/Utopian dreams
Onwards/marching
Forwards/marching
Never stop/marching
Utopia

I'm hopeful
I'm forever hopeful
I'm full of hope

Hope

Hope

Hope

Utopia

Celebrate! People of colour
Celebrate! People of the world
Celebrate humanity
Celebrate a new dawn

Free/Free from anger and hatred
Free/Free from trauma and persecution
Free/Free from bitterness and resentment
Free/Free from bigotry and tyranny

Free/to walk with you
Free/to speak openly
Free/to love who I choose
Free/to be who I want to be

Free/Free to dance with me
Free/Free to be free
We'll still have/and will always have
Tears and laughter
Failures and successes
Arguments and disagreements.
There will be moments of/anxiety and self-doubt
Moments when we feel tired/and not up for the fight
And as always/there are those that we need to take time out from!

But we've created a ripple/that's infectious
A thirst/for knowledge and wisdom
Integrity and sincerity
A trust/that works through differences
With respect, understanding and love

A tolerance/a conviction/ in the belief
That anything/and everything is possible
By working together/in unity.
So, come, let's celebrate! Celebrate!

Celebrate! People of colour
Celebrate! People of the world
Celebrate humanity
Celebrate
And rejoice

The future belongs to those who believe
in the beauty of their dreams
ELEANOR ROOSEVELT

Epilogue

To our children and their children. Less you forget

This list is not meant to be definitive or resemble some sort of hierarchical importance. These are people I've come across in my life and my search that I have admired, respected and/or who have inspired or influenced me in one way or another. Who makes your pyramid list?

Ben
Okri
Malcolm X
Samuel L Jackson
Marjorie Blackman
Bob Marley Maya
Angelou Steve Biko
Harriet Tubman Marcus
Garvey Lucky Dube Marvin
Gaye Billie Holiday Emmett Till
Hugh Masekela James Baldwin
Soledad Brothers Black Panther ANC
Chuck Berry Queen Latifah Scott Joplin
Nat King Cole Bessie Smith Gil Scott Heron
Haile Selassie Desmond Tutu Toussaint Louverture
Fidel Castro Hattie McDonald Jimmy Cliff Muhammad
Ali George Benson Dionne Warwick Eddy Grant
Rod Templeton Langston Hughes Mary Seacole Winnie
Mandela Herbie Hancock Eartha Kitt Oliver Tambo Stokely
Carmichael Madam C J Walker Rosa Parks Claudette Calvin
Katherine Johnson W E B Du Bois Nina Simone Whitney Houston
Tina Turner Viv Richards Clive Lloyd Otis Redding Toni Morrison
Frederick Douglass Sojourner Truth Barack Obama Eddy Grant Luther
Vandross Diana Ross Arrow Bryon Lee Touré Kunda Michael Jackson
Olaudah Equiano   Booker T Washington Robin Walker Carter Godwin
Woodson Isaac Hayes Curtis Mayfield James Brown Walter Rodney Sidney
Poitier Oprah Winfrey Alice Walker Phillis Wheatley Eldridge Cleaver C L R James
Stevie Wonder Josephine Baker Count Basie Al Green Louis Armstrong Jimi Hendrix
George Washington Carver Imhotep Pharaoh Khafre Khufu Sam Cooke Aretha Franklin
Charlie Parker Lewis Latimer The Real McCoy Jane C Wright George Jackson Chinua Achebe
Alex Haley Ella Baker Rebecca Lee Crumpler Dorothy Height Ray Charles Prince Muddy Waters

Bernie Grant Nelson Mandela Martin Luther King

Thanks to all the creatives who worked with me on the stage version of #Ending the Silence – for your creativity, talents and helping to refine the narrative and rhythms of some of the poems.

Francis Boua	Luke Crook
Amantha Edmead	Nomi Everall
Beverley Harry	Gill Jaggers
Derek James	Stephen Macaulay
Natty Mark-Samuels	Nicola Moses
Ehi Obhiozele	Griot Chinyere
Bawren Tavaziva	Angeli Vaid

All images - David Fisher www.fisherstudios.co.uk

Thanks and appreciation to:
Claire Thompson, Festival of the Arts, Tei Williams, Junie James & ACKHI, Pat Green, Arts at the Old Fire Station, Pegasus Theatre, Sara Lowes, David Fisher, Ben Bone, Cosima Bone

Simon and Alison North – for your eager eyes at the 11th hour

James Harrison – Publisher, for your patience and diligence

Our generous donor who wishes to remain anonymous – you know who you are.

eutondaley.com
Making Things Happen